Everyday Wonders™

It's a Sunflower!

Elisa Peters

PowerKiDS press™

New York

For Hannah Kang

Published in 2009 by The Rosen Publishing Group, Inc.
29 East 21st Street, New York, NY 10010

First Edition

Editor: Amelie von Zumbusch
Book Design: Greg Tucker
Photo Researcher: Jessica Gerweck

Photo Credits: All images by Shutterstock.com.

Library of Congress Cataloging-in-Publication Data

Peters, Elisa.
 It's a sunflower! / Elisa Peters. — 1st ed.
     p. cm. — (Everyday wonders)
 Includes index.
 ISBN 978-1-4042-4458-0 (library binding)
 1. Sunflowers—Life cycles—Juvenile literature. I. Title.
 QK495.C74P48 2009
 583'.99—dc22
                                              2007046218

Manufactured in the United States of America

Contents

Sunflowers	4
How Sunflowers Grow	10
Yummy Sunflower Seeds	18
Words to Know	24
Index	24
Web Sites	24

This beautiful flower is a sunflower.

⑤

Sunflowers have yellow **petals**.

Sunflowers are very tall.

Sunflower plants start out
as **seedlings**.

Seedlings grow tall. They form **buds** that open into flowers.

Seeds form in the center of the sunflower.

15

In time, sunflower seeds
turn black.

Birds like to eat sunflower seeds.

Lots of people eat these yummy seeds, too.

Farmers grow sunflowers and gather the plants' seeds.

Words to Know

bud

petals

seedlings

seeds

Index

B
birds, 18
buds, 12

F
farmers, 22
flower(s), 4, 12

P
petals, 6

S
seedlings, 10, 12
seeds, 14, 16, 18, 20, 22

Web Sites

Due to the changing nature of Internet links, PowerKids Press has developed an online list of Web sites related to the subject of this book. This site is updated regularly. Please use this link to access the list:

www.powerkidslinks.com/wonder/sunflower/